The
Book
of
Memories

DAVID FISHER & PATTY BROWN

A JOHN BOSWELL ASSOCIATES BOOK

~~~ A PERIGEE BOOK ~~~

Perigee Books
are published by
The Putnam Publishing Group
200 Madison Avenue
New York, NY 10016

Library of Congress Cataloging-in-Publication Data

Fisher, David.
The book of memories / by David Fisher and Patty
Brown; edited by
Elizabeth Davis.
p.   cm.
"A John Boswell Associates book."
ISBN 0-399-51599-2
1. Reminiscing—Problems, exercises, etc.   I. Brown,
Patty.
II. Davis, Elizabeth.   III. Title.
BF378.R44F57   1990   89-48848 CIP
153.1′2—dc20

Printed in the United States of America
1 2 3 4 5 6 7 8 9 10

Introduction

This is the most personal book you will ever read. In it you'll find wonderful stories about your own childhood, your days in school, people you've loved, places you've been, things you've done. This is a book that will make you smile and laugh, a book filled with the best things that ever happened to you.

It has been said that we are the sum total of our experiences and that every experience we've had in life is stored forever in our mind. When we conjure up these experiences, they are called memories.

Losing yourself in your own memories can be just about the perfect entertainment. They are gratifying, they are enjoyable, they're certainly easy to carry around, and they cost absolutely nothing (well, maybe $7.95).

This is a book filled with the most personal of all your possessions—your memories. But getting to them is going to require a little help from you. Professional actors often use their memories to help them produce an emotion they need to express the feelings of the character they're playing. When their character is happy, they simply remember something that made them happy in their own life, and that memory makes them happy again. This is where you come in. You must be willing to make the very small effort it takes to plumb the depths of your fondest and (sometimes) most distant memories.

To do this you are first going to need a question or a directed statement to help trigger a pleasant moment from your past. That's where we come in. In this book we've provided 180 triggers, 180 guided suggestions that will help bring you back to a special time or place, to a poignant moment or even a funny incident that happened many years ago.

In helping you to recall these memories we will ask you to use all of your senses.

Our senses are a storehouse of memories. We don't just think about things that happened, we remember how they looked, or smelled, or sounded or felt. We remember them by the way they made us feel. In fact, in many cases, the smell of a mother's perfume or a father's cologne, or the sound of rain on glass, or the feel of warm flannel—is enough to make us recall an entire mental picture (with ourselves in the middle).

Not every trigger in this book will apply to you, but we've attempted to select those triggers that will apply to most people. For example, we've all gone to school, had a first date, enjoyed a first kiss; we've all been scared at the movies, eaten in a luncheonette, earned our first dollar. Even when the trigger does not fire off a certain memory, what will often happen is that it will conjure up an associative memory. You may not remember the "best parade you ever went to," but that phrase might conjure up a picture of the first time you were ever in a big crowd waiting for something exciting to happen.

There are two ways to use this book. You can enjoy it sitting by yourself or you can share it with a group. Each way will bring you a different kind of pleasure.

You should keep in mind that this is not a quiz or a contest. It has nothing to do with winning or losing. There are no right or wrong answers. The only purpose of this book is to make you feel good by helping you find pleasant memories you haven't thought about in a while.

If you're alone, relax. Get really comfortable. Find yourself a great place to sit, stretch out, open up your mind. When you turn the page you'll find the first trigger. (There's one or two per page.) Read the question or suggestion, then just close your eyes and think about it.

The idea is not just to remember something, but to savor that memory, and enjoy the feeling that it provokes—the way something looked, or smelled, or sounded, the way something felt in your hand. For example, when asked to remember the meanest teacher you ever had, don't just think of him or her. For a few minutes, put yourself back in the classroom. Remember the way he or she looked and sounded, remember the particularly nasty thing that he or she did. The more time you spend with a memory, the more you really "embrace" it with all your senses, the more you'll enjoy using this book.

This book can also be used with another person or even a group. Just have someone read a question or suggestion aloud and watch what happens. The only problem is that, at first, you'll find that everyone will be shouting over one another. But soon an orderly procession of memories will take over and what you'll find is that memories of others will act as further triggers to your own memories.

Listening to other people's deepest, most personal childhood memories can also be enormously entertaining and great fun.

While compiling this book, we found working together in a group to be particularly time-consuming because of the bizarre twists the recollecting took. One of us recalled a childhood of watching TV while gnawing his way through the wooden arm of the couch. Someone else remembered going trick-or-treating for Halloween dressed as a lamp.

You will be absolutely amazed at how entertaining your mind can be, even when you're by yourself. There is a lifetime stored in your mind, just waiting to be recalled.

Pleasant memories.

—David Fisher
Patty Brown
John Boswell
Elizabeth Davis

Remember the best feeling you ever had that involved your toes?

What was the first time you felt "it doesn't get any better than this"?

3

What is your favorite picture of yourself as a child?

4

What was the hardest you ever laughed?

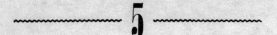

——— **5** ———

What was the best secret you ever kept?

——— **6** ———

What was the thing most difficult for you to part with?

7

Was there a time when your brother or sister or a friend was really there when you needed him or her?

8

Where was your favorite hiding place?

9

When you ran away from home, where did you go?

10

What was the most scared you ever were?

11

What was the most dramatic temper tantrum you ever threw?

12

Do you remember getting spanked?

13

What was the most embarrassing moment of your childhood?

Did you ever have a security blanket, doll, or animal?
What was its name?
How long did you have it?

15

What thing that you lost do you miss the most?
Where do you still think it is?

16

What was the most lost you ever were?

17

What did you do in your room at night when the lights were turned out?
What lights did your parents leave on?

18

What were your best bedtime stalling tactics?

19

What was the view from your bedroom window?

20

What kind of wallpaper did you have in your bedroom?

21

What did your bedspread look like?

22

What did you hang on your bedroom walls?

23

Remember the biggest storm you were ever in?

24

When were you the coldest ever in your whole life?

25

What was the best thing you ever grew yourself?

What was the biggest or ugliest bug you ever tried to kill?

Picture your first backyard.

What was the highest you ever climbed?

Remember the view looking down?

29

What did you do with the things that fell from trees?

Who was your best friend?
Who was your worst enemy?

—————— ~~~~~ **31** ~~~~~ ——————

Whose house did you and your
friends usually go to to play?

32

Whom did you give
. . . Indian burns?
. . . nugies?
. . . kooties?

33

Remember the sound of your best friend's laugh.

34

What was your most successful prank phone call?

Who was the first person outside of your immediate family that you saw stark naked?

36

Which of your friends' parents did you like best?

37

Where was your first sleep-over invitation?

38

What was the most awful thing you ever talked a friend into doing?

What was the name of your favorite pet?

What pets did you have that weren't cats or dogs?

Did you ever give your pet a funeral?

40

What was the worst thing you ever did to a pet?

Did you have a favorite candy
store?
What was your favorite
. . . candy bar?
. . . soda fountain drink?
. . . comic book?

42

What was the first magazine you ever subscribed to?

43

Who was your favorite superhero?

44

What was the brightest shining moment of your athletic career?

45

What were you going to be when you grew up?

46

What did you always want to be able to do, but never learned how to do?

47

What were some of the things you collected?

What was your favorite cereal box promotion?
What was the first thing you ever sent away for?

49

Did you ever win anything as a child?

50

Were you ever on a TV show?

ow did you learn to whistle?
. . . to snap your fingers?
. . . to blow a bubble?

Who taught you how to ride a bicycle?
What did yours look like?

Where was your favorite sledding hill?
What was your most daredevil stunt?

Who taught you to swim?

55

What was your favorite playground game?

What did you order from the ice-
cream man?
What other vendors always came to
your neighborhood?

What was your favorite type of cookie?

How did you eat your Oreo cookies?

58

What food(s) made you sick just thinking about it (them)?

59

What was your most memorable birthday party?

60

What was the best childhood present you ever received?

61

What's the strongest memory you have of the circus?

62

What was the best parade you ever went to?

63

Where did you go to see Santa Claus?

64

Where were your Christmas presents hidden?

Remember the feel of your fingers in
. . . finger paint?
. . . wet clay?
. . . papier mâché?

What did you make out of
. . . Popsicle sticks?
. . . construction paper?
. . . origami paper?

What was your best Halloween costume?

68

Remember the smell of a freshly opened box of Crayola Crayons? What was your favorite color?

What did you make out of Play-Doh that you just had to save?

What did you like to do best with
Silly Putty?

71

Did you ever own
. . . a cowboy outfit?
. . . a ballerina tutu?

What was the first song you learned to play on a musical instrument?

73

What music lessons did you take?
Did you ever perform in a recital?

What was the first movie your parents took you to see?

What was the scariest movie you ever saw?

76

Who was the first famous person
you remember meeting?
. . . Did you ask for an autograph?
. . . Do you still have it?

Which television show did you have to bargain with your parents to stay up to watch?

What was your favorite TV-watching position?
Where did you hide to watch TV when you were supposed to be in bed?

79

Remember the feeling of putting on clean pajamas after your bath?

80

What were your bathtub toys?

81

Who read you books before you went to bed?

82

What was your scariest nightmare?

83

Do you remember the smell of your mother's perfume?

84

Do you remember the smell of your father's shaving cream?

Who woke you up in the morning and how did they do it?

What special food would your mother make for you when you were sick?

87

Remember the smell of Vick's VapoRub?

88

Where did you sit at your family dinner table?

89

What was your favorite dinner?

90

Remember the smell of your favorite homemade treat?

What was Sunday morning like?
Who woke up first?
Who made breakfast?
Did your family have a Sunday routine?
What was it?

92

What is your favorite memory of Sunday School?

93

Do you remember going to a service of a different religion?

Which tablecloth did your mother save for special occasions?

Who was your most revolting relative?
Who was your favorite relative?

96

What things did a relative do that you hated the most?

97

Who carved the Thanksgiving turkey in your home?

What did the ornament at the top
of your Christmas tree look like?

Remember the sound and the smell of the family movie projector?

What was the best family vacation
you ever had?
Where did you go?
How did you get there?

Which family car do you remember the best?

Remember the first time you were in a car that broke down?

Remember the first time you were
ever on a plane?
. . . on a boat?
. . . on a train?

What restaurant did your family go to on special occasions?

What was your home telephone number?

. . . your grandparents'?

. . . your best friend's?

How was your living room decorated?

What did you do in the attic or the basement?

Did your family, your friends, or your relatives have a room you weren't allowed to play in?

What was the worst fight you ever had with a sister or brother?
. . . a friend?
. . . your parents?

— **110** —

What did your parents wear
around the house?

111

What was your favorite way to spend time alone with your mom . . . with your dad?

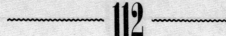

112

What was the dumbest lie you ever told your parents?

113

What was the time you were most embarrassed by your parents?

What were some of the things you found in your parents' bedroom drawers?
What did you find that you weren't supposed to find?

115

What was the angriest you ever made your parents?

116

What present do you remember making for your mom or dad?

What bad habit did your parents nag you about the most?
What was your favorite bad habit?

Which of your parents' friends did you
. . . like the most?
. . . hate the most?

Remember the voice of a favorite friend or relative who has passed away.

Who taught you to read?

What was your get-ready-for-school routine?

122

Whom did you go to school with?

123

What school supplies did you always get for the first day of school?

124

Remember the smell of
. . . white paste
. . . mimeograph paper
. . . a brand-new schoolbook?
. . . formaldehyde?

Ponder a #2 pencil.

What color were the blackboards
in your school?
What color was the chalk?

Remember the sound of a favorite teacher's voice.

What did your desk in grade school look like?
Did you sit in a special way?

129

What was the best thing you ever brought for Show & Tell?

130

What was your best school project?

131

What was the best prize you ever won?

132

What was your biggest report card problem?

133

What part did you play in your favorite class show?

134

Do you remember your favorite class trip?

What was the best lunch box you ever owned?

What did your cafeteria smell like?

What were some of the cafeteria classics?

Did you ever get sent to the principal's office?
Did you have to
. . . go to detention?
. . . sit in the corner?
. . . stand in the hallway?

138

Who was the fattest kid in your grade?

139

Who was the smartest kid in your class?

Who was your favorite teacher?
. . . the meanest?
. . . the nerdiest?
. . . the one with the worst breath?

Who was your most memorable language teacher?

What was the first thing you were ever forced to memorize?

143

How did you carry your books to and from school?

144

What do you remember about your school locker?

Who was your class hood?

What was the worst mark or grade you ever received?

147

What were your school colors?

148

What was your high-school fight song?

How did you cope with Sunday-night anxieties?

150

What was the first thing you did
when you got home from school?

What was your favorite board game?

. . . school-yard game?

. . . car game?

. . . card game?

What was your favorite after-school snack?

What was your favorite toy?
. . . trains?
. . . blocks?
. . . Legos, Etch-A-Sketch?
. . . stuffed animals?

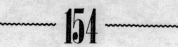

What was the dumbest hat you were forced to wear?

Do you remember your first rain-
coat?
Did it have a hood?

What was the worst haircut you ever got?

Do you remember your first piece of jewelry?

Do you remember your first watch?

What was your first doctor's name?
. . . your first dentist's?
. . . your orthodontist's?

Can you remember the taste of the space in your mouth after a tooth fell out?

Remember the feeling of the dental goop the orthodontist put in your mouth when he was making an impression?

What was the first cast you ever had to wear?
How did you scratch the itch?

What were some of the things you did to earn money?

163

What did you do to lose your allowance?

164

Remember the first time you ever opened a bank account?

Remember the most money you ever found?

What did your own first radio look like?

What were the words to the first popular song you ever knew?

What did your record player look like?

What record did you listen to more than any other you ever owned?

170

What was the first dirty word you learned and what did you think it meant?
Where did you learn it?

171

Who taught you to dance?

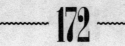

172

What was the first concert you ever went to?

173

Who told you about sex?

Who was the first person you ever
had a crush on?
Did he/she know it?

Who was the first person you ever
kissed?

What was your most memorable boy/girl party?
What kissing games did you play?

Remember the first kiss you ever had with your eyes closed.

What was the most embarrassed you have ever been on a date?

Where were you when you smoked your first cigarette?

What was the best time you had being late?